Lots to Love®
Cute As Pie
5" Doll Clothes™

Contents

Basic Pants

PATTERN NOTES

Chain-2 at beginning of both row and round counts as first half double crochet unless otherwise stated.

Join with slip stitch as indicated unless otherwise stated.

PANTS

Row 1: Beg at waist, ch 34, hdc in 3rd ch from hook *(2 sk chs do not count as first hdc)*, hdc in each rem ch across, turn. *(32 hdc)*

Rows 2 & 3: **Ch 2** *(see Pattern Notes)*, hdc in each hdc across, turn.

Rnd 4: Now working in rnds, ch 2, hdc in each hdc across, **join** *(see Pattern Notes)* in beg ch-2.

Rnd 5: Ch 2, hdc in each hdc around, join in beg ch-2 *(center back of pants)*. *(32 hdc)*

Rnd 6: Ch 2, hdc in each hdc around, join in beg ch-2.

Rnds 7 & 8: Rep rnd 6.

FIRST LEG

Rnd 9: Not counting beg ch-2 of previous rnd as a hdc, ch 2 *(for crotch)*, sk next 16 hdc, sl st in next hdc, ch 2, hdc in each of next 16 hdc, hdc in each of next 2 chs of crotch, join in ch-2. *(18 hdc)*

Rnds 10 & 11: Rep rnd 6.

Rnd 12: Ch 2, [**hdc dec** *(see Stitch Guide)* in next 2 hdc, hdc in next hdc] 6 times, join in beg ch-2. *(12 hdc)*

Rnds 13 & 14: Rep rnd 6. At the end of rnd 14, fasten off.

2ND LEG

Rnd 9: Join cotton in next unworked hdc of rnd 8, not counting beg ch-2 of previous rnd as a hdc, ch 2, hdc in each of next 16 hdc, hdc in each of next 2 chs of opposite side of foundation ch of crotch, join in beg ch-2. *(18 hdc)*

Rnds 10–14: Rep rnds 10–14 of First Leg.

With sewing needle and thread, sew snap fastener to back waistline. ●

Basic Shoes

PATTERN NOTES

Join with slip stitch as indicated unless otherwise stated.

Chain-2 at beginning of round counts as first half double crochet unless otherwise stated.

SHOES

Rnd 1: Ch 8, 2 sc in 2nd ch from hook, sc in each of next 4 chs, hdc in next ch, 4 dc in last ch, working on opposite side of foundation ch, hdc in next ch, sc in each of next 4 chs, 2 sc in the last ch, **join** (*see Pattern Notes*) in first sc. (*12 sc, 4 dc, 2 hdc*)

Rnd 2: Ch 1, 2 sc in same sc as beg ch-1, sc in each of next 5 sts, hdc in next st, 2 dc in each of next 4 sts, hdc in next st, sc in each of next 5 sts, 2 sc in next st, join in first sc. (*14 sc, 8 dc, 2 hdc*)

Rnd 3: Working in **back lp** (*see Stitch Guide*) of each st, ch 2, hdc in each st around, join in first hdc. (*24 hdc*)

Rnd 4: **Ch 2** (*see Pattern Notes*), hdc in each hdc around, join in 2nd ch of beg ch-2. (*24 hdc*)

Rnd 5: Ch 2, hdc in each of next 7 sts, [**hdc dec** (*see Stitch Guide*) in next 2 sts] 4 times, hdc in each of next 8 sts, join in 2nd ch of beg ch-2. (*20 hdc*)

Rnd 6: Ch 1, sc in each st around, join in first sc, sl st in each of next 7 sc, ch 4 (*for strap*), sk each of next 7 sc, sl st in next sc. Fasten off. ●

Strawberry *Baby*

Skill Level

EASY

Finished Size
5-inch baby doll

Materials
- Omega crochet cotton size 10 (173 yds per ball):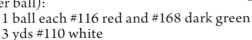
  1 ball each #116 red and #168 dark green
  3 yds #110 white
  1 yd #166 baby yellow
- Size 6/1.80mm steel crochet hook or size needed to obtain gauge
- Tapestry needle
- Sewing needle
- Matching sewing thread
- Black E beads: 53
- Size 3/0 snap fastener: 2

Gauge
8 hdc = 1 inch; 5 hdc rows = 1 inch

PATTERN NOTES
Weave in loose ends as work progresses.

Join with slip stitch as indicated unless otherwise stated.

Chain-2 at beginning of round does not count as first half double crochet unless otherwise stated.

Chain-3 at beginning of row or round counts as first double crochet unless otherwise stated.

HAT
FLOWER
Rnd 1: With baby yellow, ch 4, **join** (*see Pattern Notes*) in first ch to form a ring, **ch 2** (*see Pattern Notes*), 10 hdc in ring, join in first hdc. Fasten off.

Rnd 2: Join white in any hdc of rnd 1, ch 1, sc in first hdc, (hdc, dc, hdc) in next hdc, [sc in next hdc, (hdc, dc, hdc) in next hdc] around, join in first sc. Fasten off. (*20 sts*)

LEAVES
Make 5.

Rnd 1: With dark green, ch 11, sc in 2nd ch from hook, (hdc, dc, hdc) in next ch, [sc in next ch, (hdc, dc, hdc) in next ch] 4 times, working on opposite side of foundation ch, sc in next ch, [(hdc, dc, hdc) in next ch, sc in next ch] 4 times, join in first hdc. Leaving 4-inch length, fasten off.

HAT
Rnd 1: Beg at top of Hat with dark green, ch 4, join in first ch to form a ring, **ch 3** (*see Pattern Notes*), 7 dc in ring, join in 3rd ch of beg ch-3. (*8 dc*)

Rnd 2: Ch 3, dc in same st as beg ch-3, 2 dc in each st around, join in 3rd ch of beg ch-3. (*16 dc*)

Rnd 3: Ch 1, (sc, dc) in each dc around, join in first sc. (*32 sts*)

Rnd 4: Ch 3, sc in next dc, [dc in next sc, sc in next dc] around, join in 3rd ch of beg ch-3.

Rnd 5: Ch 1, sc in same dc as beg ch-1, dc in next sc, [sc in next dc, dc in next sc] around, join in first sc.

Rnds 6–9: [Rep rnds 4 and 5 alternately] 2 times.

Rnd 10: Ch 1, sc in each st around, join in beg sc. Fasten off.

With rem length, sew Leaves to center top of Hat. Sew Flower centered on Leaves.

DRESS

Row 1: With dark green, beg at neckline, ch 29, 2 sc in 2nd ch from hook, 2 sc in each rem ch across, turn. *(56 sc)*

Row 2: Ch 1, sc in each of first 8 sc, ch 7, sk each of next 12 sc *(armhole opening)*, sc in each of next 16 sc, ch 7, sk each of next 12 sc *(armhole opening)*, sc in each of next 8 sc, turn. *(32 sc, 2 ch-7 sps)*

Row 3: Ch 1, sc in each sc and each ch across, turn. *(46 sc)*

Row 4: Ch 3 *(see Pattern Notes)*, *[dc in next st, sc in next st] 2 times, (dc, sc) in next st, rep from * 8 times, turn. *(55 sts)*

Row 5: Ch 1, [sc in next dc, dc in next sc] across, turn.

Row 6: Ch 3, [sc in next dc, dc in next sc] across, turn.

Rows 7 & 8: Rep rows 5 and 6.

Rnd 9 (RS): Now working in rnds, ch 1, [sc in next dc, dc in next sc] around, **join** *(see Pattern Notes)* in beg sc, **do not turn**.

Rnd 10: Ch 3, [sc in each dc, dc in each sc] around, join in first st.

Rnd 11: Ch 1, [sc in each dc, dc in each sc] around, join in beg st.

Rnd 12: Ch 3, *[dc in next st, sc in next st] 2 times, maintaining pattern alternating sc and dc sts, dec over next 2 sts, rep from * 8 times, turn. *(46 sts)*

Rnd 13: Ch 1, [sc in next st, dc in next st] 4 times, dc in next st, maintaining pattern alternating sc and dc sts, dec over next 2 sts] 4 times, sc in next st, dc in next st, join in first st. *(42 sts)*

Rnds 14–19: Rep rnds 10 and 11.

Rnd 20: Ch 2 *(see Pattern Notes)*, hdc in each st around, join in first hdc. Fasten off. *(42 hdc)*

With sewing needle and thread, sew snap fastener to back neckline opening.

SEEDS
With sewing needle and thread, sew 53 E beads randomly on dress.

PANTS
Rows 1–4: With red, rep rows 1–4 of Basic Pants. *(32 hdc)*

Rnds 5–14: Now working in rnds, rep rnds 5–14 of Basic Pants.

With sewing needle and thread, sew snap fastener to back waistline. ●

Strawberry Baby

Flower Baby

Skill Level

EASY

Finished Size
5-inch baby doll

Materials
- Omega crochet cotton size 10 (173 yds per ball): **0 LACE**
  1 ball each #108 Magenta and #122 green
  25 yds #142 bright yellow
- Size 6/1.80mm steel crochet hook or size needed to obtain gauge
- Tapestry needle
- Sewing needle
- Matching sewing thread
- Size 3/0 snap fastener: 2

Gauge
8 hdc = 1 inch; 5 hdc rows = 1 inch

PATTERN NOTES
Weave in loose ends as work progresses.

Join with slip stitch as indicated unless otherwise stated.

Chain-2 at beginning of row or round does not count as first half double crochet unless otherwise stated.

BODYSUIT
PANTS
Rows 1–4: With green, rep rows 1–4 of Basic Pants. *(32 hdc)*

Rnds 5–14: Now working in rnds, rep rnds 5–14 of Basic Pants.

BODICE
Row 1: Working in opposite side of foundation ch, **join** *(see Pattern Notes)* green at back waistline, **ch 2** *(see Pattern Notes)*, [hdc in each of next 3 chs, 2 hdc in next ch] 7 times, hdc in next ch, turn. *(39 hdc)*

Row 2: Ch 2, hdc in each of next 7 hdc, ch 6, sk each of next 3 hdc *(armhole)*, hdc in each of next 19 hdc, ch 6, sk each of next 3 hdc *(armhole)*, hdc in each of next 7 hdc, turn. *(33 hdc, 2 ch-6 sps)*

Row 3: Ch 1, hdc in each of next 7 hdc, hdc in each of next 6 chs, hdc in each of next 19 hdc, hdc in each of next 6 hdc, hdc in each of next 7 hdc, turn. *(45 hdc)*

Row 4: Ch 2, [hdc in each of next 3 hdc, **hdc dec** *(see Stitch Guide)* in next 2 hdc] 9 times, **do not fasten off.** *(36 hdc)*

Row 5: Working down back opening of Bodysuit, ch 1, work 12 sc evenly sp, work 12 sc up opposite side of back opening, turn. *(24 sc)*

Row 6: Ch 1, sc in each of next 12 sc. Fasten off.

Sew snap fastener at back neck opening.

FlowerBaby

LEAF
Make 2.

Rnd 1: With green, ch 15, sc in 2nd ch from hook, sc in each of next 4 chs, hdc in each of next 4 chs, dc in each of next 4 chs, 4 tr in last ch, working on opposite side of foundation ch, dc in each of next 4 chs, hdc in each of next 4 chs, sc in each of next 5 chs, join in first sc. *(30 sts)*

Rnd 2: Ch 1, sc in each of first 5 sc, hdc in each of next 4 hdc, dc in each of next 4 dc, 2 tr in each of next 4 tr, dc in each of next 4 dc, hdc in each of next 4 hdc, sc in each of next 5 sc, join in first sc. Fasten off. *(34 sts)*

Position tr sts of rnd 2 of first leaf on left front of Bodice row 6 over 3 sts after armhole, join green, ch 1, working through both thicknesses, sc in each of next 3 sts. Fasten off.

Position tr sts of rnd 2 of 2nd leaf on right front of Bodice row 6 over 3 sts before armhole, join green, ch 1, working through both thicknesses, sc in each of next 3 sts. Fasten off.

COLLAR
Row 1: With magenta, ch 24, sc in 2nd ch from hook, sc in each rem ch across, turn. *(23 sc)*

Row 2: Ch 1, sc in first sc, [(sc, hdc, dc, hdc, sc) in next sc, sc in next sc] 11 times, turn. *(12 sc, 12 petals)*

Row 3: Ch 1, sc in first sc, [ch 5, sc in next sc between petals] 10 times, ch 5, sc in last sc, turn. *(11 ch-5 sps, 12 sc)*

Row 4: Ch 1, [(sc, hdc, 4 dc, hdc, sc) in next ch-5 sp] 11 times, turn. *(11 petals)*

Row 5: Working in back of Petal sts, sl st across to center lower edge of first petal, [ch 5, sl st at center back of next petal] 10 times, turn. *(10 ch-5 sps)*

Row 6: Ch 1, [(sc, hdc, dc, 4 tr, dc, hdc, sc) in next ch-5 sp] 10 times, turn. *(10 petals)*

Row 7: Working in back of Petal sts, sl st across to center lower edge of first petal, [ch 5, sl st at center back of next petal] 9 times, turn. *(9 ch-5 sps)*

Row 8: Ch 1, [(sc, hdc, dc, 4 tr, dc, hdc, sc) in next ch-5 sp] 9 times, turn.

Sew snap fastener at beg and end of row 1 of Collar.

FLOWER HAT
Rnd 1: With bright violet, ch 5, **join** *(see Pattern Notes)* in first ch to form a ring, **ch 2** *(see Pattern Notes)*, 10 hdc in ring, join in first hdc. *(10 hdc)*

Rnd 2: Working in back lps for remainder of Hat, ch 2, 2 hdc in each hdc around, join in first hdc. *(20 hdc)*

Rnd 3: Ch 2, [hdc in next hdc, 2 hdc in next hdc] 10 times, join in first hdc. *(30 hdc)*

Rnd 4: Ch 2, [hdc in each of next 4 hdc, 2 hdc in next hdc] 6 times, join in first hdc. *(36 hdc)*

Rnds 5–7: Ch 2, hdc in each hdc around, join in first hdc.

Rnd 8: Ch 2, [hdc in each of next 2 hdc, **hdc dec** *(see Stitch Guide)* in next 2 hdc, hdc in each of next 3 hdc, hdc dec in next 2 hdc] 4 times, join in first hdc. *(28 hdc)*

Rnd 9: Ch 1, [(sc, hdc, dc, tr, dc, hdc, sc) in next hdc, sc in next hdc] 14 times, join in beg sc. Fasten off.

Rnd 10: Join magenta in rem free lp of rnd 7, rep rnd 9.

Rnd 11: Join magenta in rem free lp of rnd 6, rep rnd 9.

FLOWER CENTER
Rnd 1: Join bright yellow in rem free lp of rnd 1 of Hat, ch 1, sc in same st as beg ch-1, [ch 3, sc in next st] around, working continuously in each rem free lp of rnds 1–4. At the end of rnd 4, fasten off. ●

Easter Egg Baby

Skill Level

■■☐☐
EASY

Finished Size
5-inch baby doll

Materials
- Omega crochet cotton size 10 (173 yds per ball):
    1 ball each #110 white and #142 bright yellow
    50 yds each #147 lilac, #120 baby pink and #164 baby blue
- Size 6/1.80mm steel crochet hook or size needed to obtain gauge
- Tapestry needle
- Sewing needle
- Matching sewing thread
- Size 3/0 snap fastener: 2

Gauge
8 hdc = 1 inch; 5 hdc rows = 1 inch

PATTERN NOTES
Weave in loose ends as work progresses.

Join with slip stitch as indicated unless otherwise stated.

Chain-2 at beginning of row or round does not count as first half double crochet unless otherwise stated.

HAT
CROWN
Rnd 1: With white, ch 4, **join** *(see Pattern Notes)* in first ch to form a ring, **ch 2** *(see Pattern Notes)*, 6 hdc in ring, join in beg hdc. *(6 hdc)*

Rnd 2: Ch 2, 2 hdc in each hdc around, join in beg ch-2. *(12 hdc)*

Rnd 3: Ch 2, [2 hdc in next hdc, hdc in next hdc] around, join in first ch-2. *(18 hdc)*

Rnd 4: Working in **back lps** *(see Stitch Guide)* for this rnd only, ch 2, [2 hdc in next hdc, hdc in next hdc] around, join in beg ch-2. *(27 hdc)*

Rnd 5: Ch 2, [hdc in each of next 2 hdc, 2 hdc in next hdc] around, join in first ch-2. *(36 hdc)*

Rnd 6: Working in back lps for this rnd only, ch 2, hdc in each hdc around, join in beg ch-2.

Rnd 7: Ch 2, hdc in each hdc around, join in beg ch-2.

Rnd 8: Rep rnd 6.

Rnd 9: Ch 1, beg in same st as beg ch-1, [sc in next st, hdc in next st, dc in next st, 2 tr in next st, dc in next st, hdc in next st] 6 times, join in beg sc. Fasten off.

Rnd 10: Join bright yellow in first sc, ch 1, sc in each st around, join in beg sc. Fasten off.

RUFFLES
Rnd 1: Working in rem free lps of rnd 3, join lilac with sc in any st, ch 3, [sc in next st, ch 3] around, join in beg sc. Fasten off.

Easter Egg Baby

Rnd 2: Working in rem free lps of rnd 5, join baby pink with sc in any st, ch 3, [sc in next st, ch 3] around, join in beg sc. Fasten off.

Rnd 3: Working in rem free lps of rnd 7, join baby blue with sc in any st, ch 3, [sc in next st, ch 3] around, join in beg sc. Fasten off.

DRESS

Row 1: Beg at neckline, with white, ch 26, sc in 2nd ch from hook, sc in each rem ch across, turn. *(25 sc)*

Row 2: Ch 2 *(see Pattern Notes)*, hdc in each sc across, turn.

Row 3: Ch 2, hdc in each of next 5 hdc, ch 7, sk next 3 hdc *(armhole)*, hdc in each of next 9 hdc, ch 7, sk next 3 hdc *(armhole)*, hdc in each of next 5 hdc, turn. *(19 hdc, 2 ch-7 sps)*

Row 4 (RS): Working in **back lps** *(see Stitch Guide)* for this row only, ch 2, hdc in first st, [2 hdc in next st, hdc in next st] 16 times, turn. *(49 hdc)*

Row 5: Ch 2, hdc in each hdc across, turn.

Row 6: Working in back lps for this row only, ch 2, hdc in first hdc, [2 hdc in next hdc, hdc in next hdc] across, turn. *(73 hdc)*

Row 7: Rep row 5.

Rnd 8 (RS): Now working in rnds, working in back lps for this rnd only, ch 2, hdc in each hdc around, **join** *(see Pattern Notes)* in first hdc, **do not turn.**

Rnd 9: Ch 2, hdc in each hdc around, join in first hdc.

Rnd 10: Working in back lps for this rnd only, ch 2, hdc in each hdc around, join in first hdc.

Rnd 11: Ch 2, [hdc in each of next 4 hdc, **hdc dec** *(see Stitch Guide)* in next 2 hdc] 12 times, join in first hdc. *(61 hdc)*

Rnd 12: Working in back lps for this rnd only, ch 2, [hdc in each of next 3 hdc, hdc dec in next 2 hdc] 12 times, join in beg ch-2. *(49 hdc)*

Rnd 13: Ch 2, hdc in each of next 3 hdc, [hdc dec in next 2 hdc, hdc in each of next 4 hdc] 7 times, join in beg ch-2. *(42 hdc)*

Rnd 14: Working in back lps for this rnd only, ch 2, hdc in each of next 4 hdc, hdc dec in next 2 hdc, [hdc in each of next 5 hdc, hdc dec in next 2 hdc] 5 times, join in beg ch-2. *(36 hdc)*

Rnd 15: Ch 1, beg in same st as beg ch-1, [sc in next st, hdc in next st, dc in next st, 2 tr in next st, dc in next st, hdc in next st] 6 times, join in beg sc. Fasten off.

Rnd 16: Join yellow in first sc, ch 1, sc in same st, sc in each st around, working 2 sc in sp between tr sts, join in beg sc. Fasten off.

BACK OPENING

Row 1: Join white in opposite side of foundation ch of right back opening of neckline, ch 1, work 11 sc evenly sp down back opening, do not turn, work 11 sc evenly sp up left back opening to neckline edge, turn.

Row 2: Ch 1, sc in each of next 11 sc of left back opening. Fasten off.

Sew snap fastener at back neck opening.

RUFFLES

Row 1: Join lilac in first rem free lp of row 3, ch 1, sc in same st as beg ch-1, [ch 3, sc in next st] across. Fasten off.

Row 2: Join baby pink in first rem free lp of row 5, ch 1, sc in same st as beg ch-1, [ch 3, sc in next st] across. Fasten off.

Row 3: Join baby blue in first rem free lp of row 7, ch 1, sc in same st as beg ch-1, [ch 3, sc in next st] across. Fasten off.

Rnd 4: Now working in rnds, join bright yellow in first rem free lp of rnd 9, ch 1, sc in same st as beg ch-1, ch 3, [sc in next st, ch 3] around, join in first sc. Fasten off.

Rnd 5: Join lilac in first rem free lp of rnd 11, ch 1, sc in same st as beg ch-1, ch 3, [sc in next st, ch 3] around, join in first sc. Fasten off.

Rnd 6: Join baby pink in first rem free lp of rnd 13, ch 1, sc in same st as beg ch-1, ch 3, [sc in next st, ch 3] around, join in first sc. Fasten off.

BLOOMERS

Row 1 (WS): Beg at waistline, with bright yellow, ch 40, hdc in 3rd ch from hook *(2 sk chs do not count as hdc)*, hdc in each rem ch across, turn. *(38 hdc)*

Rows 2–4: **Ch 2** *(see Pattern Notes)*, hdc in each hdc across, turn.

Rnd 5 (RS): Now working in rnds, ch 2, hdc in each hdc across, **join** *(see Pattern Notes)* in first hdc, **do not turn.**

Rnd 6: Ch 2, hdc in each hdc around, join in first hdc.

Rnd 7: Rep rnd 5.

FIRST LEG OPENING

Rnd 8: Ch 2, sk next 18 hdc, sl st in next hdc *(to form crotch)*, ch 2, hdc in same hdc as ch-2, hdc in each of next 18 hdc, hdc in next hdc, hdc in each of next 2 chs of crotch, join in first hdc. Fasten off. *(22 hdc)*

2ND LEG OPENING

Rnd 8: Join bright yellow in next unworked hdc of rnd 6 at center back of Bloomers, ch 2, hdc in same hdc, hdc in each of next 18 hdc, hdc in next hdc at center, hdc in each of next 2 chs of opposite side of crotch, hdc in next hdc, join in first hdc. Fasten off. *(22 hdc)*

Sew snap fastener at back waistline of Bloomers.

SHOE
Make 2.

Rnd 1: With white, ch 8, 2 sc in 2nd ch from hook, sc in each of next 4 chs, hdc in next ch, 4 dc in last ch, working on opposite side of foundation ch, hdc in next ch, sc in each of next 4 chs, 2 sc in same ch as beg 2-sc, **join** *(see Pattern Notes)* in beg sc. *(12 sc, 4 dc, 2 hdc)*

Rnd 2: Ch 1, 2 sc in first sc, sc in each of next 5 sc, hdc in next hdc, 2 dc in each of next 4 dc, hdc in next hdc, sc in each of next 5 sc, 2 sc in last sc, join in first sc. *(14 sc, 8 dc, 2 hdc)*

Rnd 3: Working in **back lps** *(see Stitch Guide)*, ch 1, sc in each st around, join in first sc. *(24 sc)*

Rnd 4: Ch 1, sc in each sc around, join in first sc.

Rnd 5: Ch 1, sc in each of next 9 sc, [**sc dec** *(see Stitch Guide)* in next 2 sc] 3 times, sc in each of next 9 sc, join in beg sc. *(21 sc)*

Rnd 6: Ch 1, sc in each of next 7 sc, [sc dec in next 2 sc] 3 times, sc in each of next 8 sc, join in beg sc. *(18 sc)*

Rnd 7: Ch 1, [sc in next sc, hdc in next sc, dc in next sc, 2 tr in next sc, dc in next sc, hdc in next sc] 3 times, join in first sc. Fasten off. *(21 sts)*

Rnd 8: Join bright yellow at center back of Shoe, ch 1, sc in each st around, join in first sc. Fasten off. *(21 sc)* ●

Butterfly *Baby*

Skill Level

EASY

Finished Size
5-inch baby doll

Materials
- Omega crochet cotton size 10 (173 yds per ball):
  1 ball #127 black
  50 yds each #102 wine and #137 aqua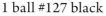
- Size 6/1.80mm steel crochet hook or size needed to obtain gauge
- Tapestry needle
- Sewing needle
- Matching sewing thread
- Black chenille stem
- 3/0 snap fastener: 1

Gauge
8 hdc = 1 inch; 5 hdc rows = 1 inch

PATTERN NOTES
Weave in loose ends as work progresses.

Join with slip stitch as indicated unless otherwise stated.

Chain-2 at beginning of row or round does not count as first half double crochet unless otherwise stated.

Chain-3 at beginning of row or round does not count as first double crochet unless otherwise stated.

BODYSUIT
RIGHT FOOT & LEG
Rnd 1: With black, ch 8, 2 sc in 2nd ch from hook, sc in each of next 4 chs, hdc in next ch, 4 dc in next ch, working on opposite side of foundation ch, hdc in next ch, sc in each of next 4 chs, 2 sc in same ch as first 2 sc, **join** *(see Pattern Notes)* in first sc. *(18 sts)*

Rnd 2: Ch 1, 2 sc in first sc, sc in each of next 5 sc, hdc in next hdc, 2 dc in each of next 4 dc, hdc in next hdc, sc in each of next 5 sc, 2 sc in next sc, join in first sc. *(24 sts)*

Rnd 3: Ch 1, working in **back lp** *(see Stitch Guide)* for this rnd only, sc in each st around, join in first sc. *(24 sc)*

Rnd 4: Ch 1, sc in each of first 8 sts, [**sc dec** *(see Stitch Guide)* over next 2 sts] 4 times, sc in each of next 8 sts, join in first sc. *(20 sc)*

Rnd 5: Ch 1, sc in each of first 7 sc, [sc dec over next 2 sc] 3 times, sc in each of next 7 sc, join in first sc. *(17 sc)*

Rnd 6: Ch 2 *(see Pattern Notes)*, hdc in first st, [2 hdc in next st, hdc in next st] 8 times, join in first hdc. *(25 hdc)*

Rnds 7–9: Ch 3 *(see Pattern Notes)*, dc in each st around, join in 3rd ch of beg ch-3. At the end of rnd 9, fasten off. *(25 dc)*

LEFT FOOT & LEG
Rnds 1–9: Rep rnds 1–9 of Right Foot & Leg. At the end of rnd 9, **do not fasten off.**

BODY

Rnd 10: With toe of each Foot pointing forward, fold Leg flat across, ch 3, dc across to center front of leg, working on rem Leg, dc in each dc around, dc in each rem dc of first Leg, join in 3rd ch of beg ch-3. *(50 dc)*

Rnd 11: With toes pointing forward, sl st to center back of Bodysuit, ch 3, dc in each dc around, join in 3rd ch of beg ch-3.

Rnd 12: Ch 3, dc in each dc around, join in beg ch-3.

Row 13: Now working in rows, ch 3, dc in each of next 49 dc, **do not join**, turn.

Row 14: Ch 3, dc in each dc across, turn.

Row 15: Ch 3, dc in each of next 11 dc, ch 7, sk next 4 dc *(armhole)*, dc in each of next 18 dc, ch 7, sk next 4 dc *(armhole)*, dc in each of next 12 dc, turn. *(42 dc, 2 ch-7 sps)*

Row 16: Ch 3, dc in next dc, **dc dec** *(see Stitch Guide)* over next 2 dc, [dc in each of next 2 dc, dc dec over next 2 dc] 13 times, turn. *(42 dc)*

Row 17: Ch 3, dc in next dc, [dc dec over next 2 dc, dc in each of next 2 dc] 10 times, turn. *(32 dc)*

Row 18: Ch 1, sc in each of next 32 dc, work 12 sc evenly sp down back opening, work 12 sc up opposite side of back opening. Fasten off.

Sew snap fastener at back neckline opening.

WING
Make 2.

Row 1: With wine, ch 12, hdc in 2nd ch from hook, hdc in each of next 6 chs, sc in each of next 4 chs, turn. *(11 sts)*

Row 2: Ch 1, sc in each of first 2 sts, 2 sc in next st, sc in next st, dc in each of next 7 sts, turn. *(12 sts)*

Row 3: **Ch 3** *(see Pattern Notes)*, dc in each of next 6 sts, sc in each of next 5 sts, turn. *(12 sts)*

Row 4: Ch 1, sc in each of first 2 sts, 2 hdc in next st, sc in each of next 2 sts, dc in each of next 3 sts, 2 dc in next st, dc in each of next 2 sts, 2 dc in last st, turn. *(15 sts)*

Row 5: Ch 3, dc in same st as beg ch-3, dc in each of next 8 sts, sc in each of next 2 sts, 2 hdc in each of next 2 sts, sc in next st, 2 sc in next st, turn. *(19 sts)*

Row 6: Ch 1, sc in each of first 7 sts *(bottom of Wing)*, dc in each of next 12 sts, do not turn. Fasten off. *(19 sts)*

Row 7: **Join** *(see Pattern Notes)* aqua in opposite side of foundation ch at bottom of Wing, ch 1, work 7 sc evenly sp across bottom edge of Wing, sc in each of next 19 sts of row 6, work 12 sc evenly sp in ends of rows across top of Wing, ending with last sc in opposite side of foundation ch, turn. *(38 sc)*

Row 8: **Ch 2** *(see Pattern Notes)*, hdc in each of first 12 sc, 3 hdc in next sc, hdc in each of next 10 sc, sc in each of next 2 sc, hdc in each of next 5 sc, 3 hdc in next sc, hdc in each of next 7 sc, turn. *(42 sts)*

Row 9: Ch 2, hdc in each of first 8 sts, 3 hdc in next st, hdc in each of next 5 sts, sc in each of next 3 sts, hdc in each of next 11 sts, 3 hdc in next st, hdc in each of next 13 sts. Fasten off. *(46 sts)*

Rnd 10: Now working in rnds, join black in last st of row 9 at top of Wing, ch 1, sc in same st as beg ch-1, [ch 3, sc in next st] rep in each st of row 9, working on inner edge of Wing, work 19 sc evenly sp up edge to top of Wing, join in beg sc. Fasten off.

Starting at neckline, position the 19 sc worked on inner edge of Wing down back opening, sew 19 sc to back of Bodysuit. Sew 2nd Wing to opposite edge of back opening.

HAT
Rnd 1: Beg at top of Hat, with black, ch 4, **join** *(see Pattern Notes)* in first ch to form a ring, **ch 2** *(see Pattern Notes)*, 8 hdc in ring, join in first hdc.

Butterfly Baby

Rnd 2: Ch 2, 2 hdc in each hdc around, join in first hdc. *(16 hdc)*

Rnd 3: Ch 2, hdc in each hdc around, join in first hdc.

Rnd 4: Rep rnd 3.

Rnd 5: Rep rnd 2. *(32 hdc)*

Rnds 6–9: Rep rnd 3.

Rnd 10: Ch 1, sc in each hdc around, join in first sc. Fasten off.

ANTENNAS

Cut chenille stem to measure 5 inches. With care, pass end of chenille stem through st at side edge of rnd 5 and out opposite side edge through rnd 5. With equal lengths on each side of Hat, push center of stem to inside top of Hat. *(Optional: Tack stem in place at center inside of Hat.)* Using photo as a guide, bend outer edges of stem upward and curl each end of stem in a circle, forming the curl of each end of the Antenna. ●

Pumpkin Baby

Skill Level

EASY

Finished Size

5-inch baby doll

Materials

- Omega crochet cotton size 10 (173 yds per ball):
    1 ball each #149 bright mango and #122 green
- Size 6/1.80mm steel crochet hook or size needed to obtain gauge
- Tapestry needle
- Sewing needle
- Matching sewing thread
- Size 3/0 snap fastener: 2

Gauge

8 hdc = 1 inch; 5 hdc rows = 1 inch

PATTERN NOTES

Weave in loose ends as work progresses.

Chain-3 at beginning of row or round counts as first double crochet unless otherwise stated.

Join with slip stitch as indicated unless otherwise stated.

Chain-2 at beginning of round does not count as first half double crochet unless otherwise stated.

BODYSUIT

Row 1 (RS): Beg at neckline, with bright mango, ch 29, 2 sc in 2nd ch from hook, 2 sc in each rem ch across, turn. *(56 sc)*

Row 2: Ch 1, sc in each sc across, turn.

Row 3: Ch 1, sc in each of first 8 sc, ch 7, sk each of next 12 sc *(armhole opening)*, sc in each of next 16 sc, ch 7, sk each of next 12 sc *(armhole opening)*, sc in each of next 8 sc, turn. *(32 sc, 2 ch-7 sps)*

Row 4: **Ch 3** *(see Pattern Notes)*, dc in each of next 7 sc, dc in each of next 7 chs, dc in each of next 16 sc, dc in each of next 7 chs, dc in each of next 8 sc, turn. *(46 dc)*

Row 5 (RS): Ch 3, dc in each of next 3 dc, [**fpdc** *(see Stitch Guide)* around next dc, dc in next dc, 2 dc in next dc, dc in next dc] 9 times, fpdc around next dc, dc in each of next 4 dc, fpdc around next dc, **join** *(see Pattern Notes)* in 3rd ch of beg ch-3, **do not turn**. *(44 dc, 12 fpdc)*

Rnd 6: Now working in rnds, ch 3, dc in each of next 3 dc, dc in top of next fpdc, fpdc around same fpdc, [dc in each of next 4 dc, dc in top of next fpdc, fpdc around same fpdc] around, join in beg ch-3. *(55 dc, 12 fpdc)*

Rnd 7: Ch 3, dc in each of next 4 dc, fpdc around next fpdc, [dc in each of next 5 dc, fpdc around next fpdc] around, join in beg ch-3.

Rnd 8: Ch 3, dc in next dc, **dc dec** *(see Stitch Guide)* over next 2 dc, dc in next dc, fpdc around next fpdc, [dc in each of next 2 dc, dc dec over next 2 dc, dc in next dc, fpdc around next fpdc] around, join in beg ch-3. *(44 dc, 12 fpdc)*

Rnd 9: Ch 3, dc in each of next 3 dc, fpdc around next dc, [dc in each of next 4 dc, fpdc around next fpdc] around, join in beg ch-3.

Rnds 10 & 11: Rep rnd 9.

Rnd 12: Ch 1, [sc in each of next 2 dc, **sc dec** (see Stitch Guide) in next 2 dc] around, join in beg sc. Fasten off. (42 sc)

SLEEVE
Make 2.

Row 1: Working sk sts of row 3 of Bodysuit, with RS facing, join green in first sk sc, ch 1, sk sc that ch-1 was worked, sc in each of next 11 sc, turn. (11 sc)

Row 2: Ch 1, sk first sc, (sc, hdc, dc, hdc, sc) in next sc, [sk next sc, (sc, hdc, dc, hdc, sc) in next sc] 4 times, sl st in last sc. Fasten off. (5 petals)

BACK OPENING
With RS facing, join bright mango with sc in side edge of row 1 of back opening, sc evenly sp down back opening and up opposite edge. Fasten off.

Sew snap fastener to back neckline opening.

HAT
Rnd 1: With bright mango, ch 5, **join** (see Pattern Notes) in first ch to form a ring, **ch 3** (see Pattern Notes), 11 dc in ring, join in beg ch-3. (12 dc)

Rnd 2: Ch 3, dc in same dc as beg ch-3, **fpdc** (see Stitch Guide) around next dc, [2 dc in next dc, fpdc around next dc] around, join in beg ch-3. (12 dc, 6 fpdc)

Rnd 3: Ch 3, 2 dc in next dc, fpdc around next dc, [dc in next dc, 2 dc in next dc, fpdc around next dc] around, join in beg ch-3. (18 dc, 6 fpdc)

Rnd 4: Ch 3, dc in next 2 dc, dc in top of fpdc, fpdc around same fpdc, [dc in each of next 3 dc, dc in top of next fpdc, fpdc around same fpdc] around, join in beg ch-3. (24 dc, 6 fpdc)

Rnd 5: Ch 3, dc in each of next 3 dc, fpdc around next fpdc, [dc in each of next 4 dc, fpdc around next fpdc] around, join in beg ch-3. (24 dc, 6 fpdc)

Rnd 6: Ch 3, dc in next dc, 2 dc in next dc, dc in next dc, fpdc around next fpdc, [dc in each of next 2 dc, 2 dc in next dc, dc in next dc, fpdc around next fpdc] around, join in beg ch-3. (30 dc, 6 fpdc)

Rnd 7: Ch 3, dc in each of next 4 dc, fpdc around next fpdc, [dc in each of next 5 dc, fpdc around next fpdc] around, join in beg ch-3.

Rnd 8: Ch 1, sc in each st around, join in beg sc. Fasten off. (36 sc)

STEM
Rnd 1: With green, ch 4, join in first ch to form a ring, **ch 2** (see Pattern Notes), work 10 hdc in ring, join in first hdc. (10 hdc)

Rnd 2: Working in **back lp** (see Stitch Guide), ch 2, hdc in each st around, join in first hdc.

Rnds 3 & 4: Ch 2, hdc in each hdc around, join in first hdc. At the end of rnd 4, leaving 8-inch length, fasten off.

VINE
Make 7.

Row 1: With green, ch 11, 2 sc in 2nd ch from hook, 2 sc in each rem ch across. Leaving 8-inch length, fasten off.

Sew 1 Vine to base of Hat Stem.

PANTS
Rows 1–4: With bright mango, rep rows 1–4 of Basic Pants. (32 hdc)

Rnds 5–14: Now working in rnds, rep rnds 5–14 of Basic Pants.

With sewing needle and thread, sew snap fastener to back waistline.

SHOE
Make 2.

Rnds 1–6: With green, rep rnds 1–6 of Basic Shoes.

Sew 1 Vine to each side of Shoe Strap and 1 at center back of Shoe. ●

Pumpkin Baby

Gingerbread Baby

Gingerbread *Baby*

Skill Level

EASY

Finished Size
5-inch baby doll

Materials
- Omega crochet cotton size 10 (173 yds per ball):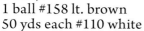
    1 ball #158 lt. brown
    50 yds each #110 white
- Size 6/1.80mm steel crochet hook or size needed to obtain gauge
- Tapestry needle
- Sewing needle
- Matching sewing thread
- Size 3/0 snap fastener: 2
- 4mm shank buttons: 8

Gauge
8 hdc = 1 inch; 5 hdc rows = 1 inch

PATTERN NOTES
Weave in loose ends as work progresses.

Join with slip stitch as indicated unless otherwise stated.

Chain-2 at beginning of row or round does not counts as first half double crochet unless otherwise stated.

HAT
Rnd 1: Starting at center top of Hat, with lt. brown, ch 5, **join** (*see Pattern Notes*) to form a ring, ch 1, 10 sc in ring, join in first sc.

Rnd 2: Ch 1, (sc, hdc) in each sc around, join in first sc. (*20 sts*)

Rnd 3: Rep rnd 2. (*40 sts*)

Rnd 4: Ch 1, [sc in each hdc, hdc in each sc] around, join in first st.

Rnd 5: Rep rnd 4.

Rnd 6: Ch 1, [hdc in next st, sc in next st, hdc in next st, sc in next st, (hdc, sc) in next st] 8 times, join in first st. (*48 sts*)

Rnd 7: Rep rnd 4.

Rnd 8: Working in **back lp** (*see Stitch Guide*) of sts, ch 1, [sc in each hdc, hdc in each sc] around, join in beg st.

Rnd 9: Rep rnd 4.

Rnd 10: Ch 1, *[sc in next hdc, hdc in next sc] 3 times, sc dec in next 2 sts, rep from * around, join in beg st. (*42 sts*)

Rnd 11: Ch 1, sc in each st around, join in first st. Fasten off.

Rnd 12: Join white with sc in any sc of rnd 11, sc in each rem sc around, join in first st. Fasten off. (*42 sc*)

BRIM

Rnd 1: Working in rem free lps of rnd 7, join white with sc in any st, ch 3, [sc in next st, ch 3] around, join in beg sc. Fasten off.

With sewing needle and thread, sew 3 buttons to rnd 1 of center top of Hat.

PANTS

Row 1: With lt. brown, ch 38, hdc in 3rd ch from hook (*2 sk chs do not count as first hdc*), hdc in each rem ch across, turn. (*36 hdc*)

Row 2: **Ch 2** (*see Pattern Notes*), hdc in each hdc across, turn.

Rnd 3: Now working in rnds, ch 1, hdc in each hdc across, **join** (*see Pattern Notes*) in first hdc, **do not turn.**

Rnd 4: Ch 2, hdc in each hdc around, join in first hdc.

Rnds 5–7: Rep rnd 4.

FIRST LEG

Rnd 8: Mark center front st, ch 2 (*for crotch*), sl st in center front st, ch 2, hdc in each hdc around Leg opening, hdc in each of 2 chs, join in first hdc. (*20 hdc*)

Rnds 9–11: Rep rnd 4.

Rnd 12: Ch 2, [hdc in each of next 2 hdc, **hdc dec** (*see Stitch Guide*) over next 2 hdc] 5 times, join in first hdc. (*15 hdc*)

Rnd 13: Rep rnd 4. Fasten off.

Rnd 14: Join white with sc in any hdc, ch 3, [sc in next hdc, ch 3] around, join in first sc. Fasten off.

2ND LEG

Rnd 8: Join lt. brown in next unworked st of rnd 7, ch 2, hdc in each hdc around, hdc in each ch of ch-2 sp of crotch, join in first hdc. (*20 hdc*)

Rnds 9–14: Rep rnds 9–14 of First Leg.

With sewing needle and thread, sew snap fastener to back opening of waistline.

TOP

Row 1: Beg at neckline, with lt. brown, ch 29, 2 sc in 2nd ch from hook, 2 sc in each rem ch across, turn. (*56 sc*)

Row 2: **Ch 2** (*see Pattern Notes*), working in **back lp** (*see Stitch Guide*), hdc in each st across, turn.

Row 3: Ch 2, [hdc in next st, sc in next st] 5 times, ch 6, sk next 8 sts (*armhole opening*), [hdc in next st, sc in next st] 10 times, ch 6, sk next 8 sts (*armhole opening*), [hdc in next st, sc in next st] 5 times, turn. (*40 sts, 2 ch-6 sps*)

Row 4: Ch 2, [hdc in next sc, sc in next hdc] 5 times, [hdc in next ch, sc in next ch] 3 times, [hdc in next sc, sc in next hdc] 10 times, [hdc in next ch, sc in next ch] 3 times, [hdc in next sc, sc in next hdc] 5 times, turn. (*52 sts*)

Row 5: Ch 2, hdc in first st, [sc in next hdc, hdc in next sc] 6 times, (sc, hdc, sc) in next hdc, hdc in next sc, [sc in next hdc, hdc in next sc] 11 times, (sc, hdc, sc) in next hdc, [hdc in next sc, sc in next hdc] 7 times, turn. (*56 sts*)

Rows 6–8: Ch 2, hdc in each sc and sc in each hdc across, turn.

Row 9: Ch 2, hdc in each sc and sc in each hdc, ending with 2 sts in last st, turn. (*57 sts*)

Row 10: Ch 1, sc in first st, sk next st, 5 dc in next st, sk next st, sc in next st] 14 times. Fasten off. (*14 groups 5-dc, 15 sc*)

BOTTOM TRIM

Row 11: **Join** (*see Pattern Notes*) white with sc in first sc, [ch 3, sc in next st] across. Fasten off.

SLEEVE
Make 2.

Rnd 1: Join lt. brown at center underarm, ch 1, work 16 sc evenly sp around, join in beg sc.

Rnd 2: Ch 2, hdc in first st, [sc in next st, hdc in next st] 2 times, [(sc, hdc) in next st] 6 times, [sc in next st, hdc in next st] 2 times, sc in next st, join in first hdc. (*22 sts*)

Rnd 3: Ch 1, [sc in next hdc, hdc in next sc] around, join in first sc.

Rnd 4: Ch 2, [hdc in next sc, sc in next hdc] around, join in first hdc.

Rnds 5 & 6: Ch 1, [sc in next st, hdc in next st] around, dec 3 sts evenly sp around, join in first st. *(16 sts)*

Rnds 7 & 8: Rep rnd 3.

Rnd 9: Ch 1, sc in each st around, join in first sc. Fasten off.

Rnd 10: Join white with sc in first st, ch 3, [sc in next st, ch 3] around, join in first sc. Fasten off.

NECKLINE TRIM
Row 1: Join white with sc in rem free lp of row 1 of Top, [ch 3, sc in next st] across. Fasten off.

With sewing needle and thread, sew snap fastener at back neckline edge.

Sew 3 buttons evenly sp down center front of Top.

SHOE
Make 2.

Rnds 1–6: With lt. brown, rep rnds 1–6 of Basic Shoes.

With sewing needle and thread, sew a button to center front of Shoe between rnds 5 and 6. ●

Christmas Tree Baby

Christmas Tree *Baby*

Skill Level

◼◼◻◻
EASY

Finished Size
5-inch baby doll

Materials
- Omega crochet cotton size 10 (173 yds per ball):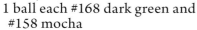
  1 ball each #168 dark green and #158 mocha
  2 yds #142 bright yellow
- Size 6/1.80mm steel crochet hook or size needed to obtain gauge
- Tapestry needle
- Sewing needle
- Matching sewing thread
- Size 3/0 snap fastener: 2
- 4mm shank buttons: 79

Gauge
8 hdc = 1 inch; 5 hdc rows = 1 inch

PATTERN NOTES
Weave in loose ends as work progresses.

Chain-3 at beginning of row or round counts as first double crochet unless otherwise stated.

Join with slip stitch as indicated unless otherwise stated.

Chain-2 at beginning of round does not count as first half double crochet unless otherwise stated.

SPECIAL STITCH
Scallop: (Sc, hdc, dc, ch 1, dc, hdc, sc) in indicated st.

DRESS
Row 1: With dark green, beg at neckline, ch 29, 2 sc in 2nd ch from hook, 2 sc in each rem ch across, turn. *(56 sc)*

Row 2: Ch 1, sc in each of next 8 sc, ch 7, sk each of next 12 sc *(armhole opening)*, sc in each of next 16 sc, ch 7, sk each of next 12 sc *(armhole opening)*, sc in each of next 8 sc, turn. *(32 sc, 2 ch-7 sps)*

Row 3: Ch 1, sc in each sc and each ch across, turn. *(46 sc)*

Row 4: Working in **back lp** *(see Stitch Guide)* for this row only, **ch 3** *(see Pattern Notes)*, dc in each of next 2 dc, [2 dc in next dc, dc in each of next 3 dc] 10 times, 2 dc in next dc, dc in each of next 2 dc, turn. *(57 dc)*

Row 5: Ch 3, dc in each dc across, turn.

Row 6: Working in back lp of each st, ch 3, dc in each of next 3 dc, [2 dc in next dc, dc in each of next 4 dc] 10 times, 2 dc in next dc, dc in each of next 2 dc, turn. *(68 dc)*

Rnd 7 (RS): Now working in rnds, ch 3, dc in each dc across, **join** *(see Pattern Notes)* in 3rd ch of beg ch-3, **do not turn.**

Rnd 8: Working in back lp of each st, ch 3, dc in each st around, join in beg ch-3.

Rnd 9: Ch 3, dc in each st around, join in beg ch-3.

Rnd 10: Working in back lp of each st, ch 3, dc in each of next 4 dc, [2 dc in next dc, dc in each of next 5 dc] 10 times, 2 dc in next dc, dc in each of next 2 dc, turn. *(79 dc)*

Rnd 11: Rep rnd 9.

Rnd 12: Ch 1, sc in first st, [**scallop** *(see Special Stitch)* in next st, sc in next st] around, join in first sc. Fasten off. *(39 scallops, 40 sc)*

SCALLOP
Row 1: Join dark green with sc in first rem free lp of row 3, [scallop in next st, sc in next st] across row. Fasten off.

Row 2: Rep row 1 in rem free lps of row 5.

Rnd 3: Join dark green with sc in first rem st of rnd 7, [scallop in next st, sc in next st] around, join in first sc. Fasten off.

Rnd 4: Rep rnd 3 in rem free lps of rnd 9.

NECKLINE SCALLOP
Row 1: With WS facing, join dark green in first ch of opposite side of foundation ch, ch 1, sc in next ch, sk next ch, scallop in next ch, sk next ch, sc in next ch, scallop in next ch, sk next ch, [sc in next ch, scallop in next ch] 6 times, sc in next ch, sk next ch, scallop in next ch, sc in next ch, sk next ch, scallop in next ch, sk next ch, sc in next ch. Fasten off. *(10 scallops, 11 sc)*

BACK OPENING
Join dark green at back neckline, ch 1, sc evenly sp down back opening and up opposite edge of opening. Fasten off.

With sewing needle and thread, sew snap fastener to back neckline opening.

DECORATIVE LIGHTS
With sewing needle and thread, randomly sew 57 buttons on Scallops of Dress.

HAT
Rnd 1: Starting at top of Hat with dark green, ch 4, **join** *(see Pattern Notes)* in first ch, **ch 2** *(see Pattern Notes)*, 8 hdc in ring, join in first hdc.

Rnd 2: Ch 2, work 2 hdc in each hdc around, join in first hdc. *(16 hdc)*

Rnd 3: Working in back lp of each st for this rnd only, ch 2, hdc in each st around, join in first hdc.

Rnd 4: Ch 2, [hdc in next hdc, 2 hdc in next hdc] around, join in first hdc. *(24 hdc)*

Rnd 5: Rep rnd 3.

Rnd 6: Rep rnd 4. *(36 hdc)*

Rnd 7: Rep rnd 3.

Rnd 8: Ch 2, hdc in each of next 3 sts, [2 hdc in next st, hdc in each of next 2 sts] 10 times, hdc in each of next 3 sts, join in first hdc. *(46 hdc)*

Rnd 9: Rep rnd 3.

Rnd 10: Ch 2, hdc in each hdc around, join in first hdc.

Rnd 11: Ch 1, sc in each hdc around, join in first sc. *(46 sc)*

Rnd 12: Ch 1, sc in first sc, scallop in next sc, [sc in next sc, scallop in next sc] 22 times, join in first sc. Fasten off. *(23 scallops, 23 sc)*

SCALLOP
Rnd 1: Join dark green with sc in first rem lp of rnd 2, [scallop in next st, sc in next st] around, join in first sc. Fasten off.

Rnd 2: Rep rnd 1 in rem free lps of rnd 4.

Rnd 3: Rep rnd 1 in rem free lps of rnd 6.

Rnd 4: Rep rnd 1 in rem free lps of rnd 8.

STAR

Rnd 1: With bright yellow, **ch 3** (*see Pattern Notes*), join in first ch to form a ring, ch 1, 6 sc in ring, join in first sc.

Rnd 2: Ch 1, (sc, 2 dc, sc) in each sc around, join in first sc. Fasten off. (*24 sts*)

DECORATIVE LIGHTS

With sewing needle and thread, randomly sew 22 buttons on rnds 1–4 of Scallops of Hat. Do not sew any buttons on rnd 12 of Hat.

PANTS

Rows 1–4: With mocha, rep rows 1–4 of Basic Pants. (*32 hdc*)

Rnds 5–14: Now working in rnds, rep rnds 5–14 of Basic Pants.

With sewing needle and thread, sew snap fastener to back waistline.

SHOE
Make 2.

Rnds 1–6: With mocha, rep rnds 1–6 of Basic Shoes. ●

STITCH GUIDE

FOR MORE COMPLETE INFORMATION, VISIT **ANNIESCATALOG.COM/STITCHGUIDE**

STITCH ABBREVIATIONS

beg . . . . begin/begins/beginning
bpdc . . . . back post double crochet
bpsc . . . . .back post single crochet
bptr . . . . .back post treble crochet
CC . . . . .contrasting color
ch(s) . . . . .chain(s)
ch- . . . . refers to chain or space
previously made (i.e., ch-1 space)
ch sp(s) . . . . chain space(s)
cl(s) . . . . cluster(s)
cm . . . . centimeter(s)
dc . . . . .double crochet (singular/plural)
dc dec . . . . double crochet 2 or more
stitches together, as indicated
dec . . . . .decrease/decreases/decreasing
dtr . . . . double treble crochet
ext . . . . .extended
fpdc . . . . front post double crochet
fpsc . . . . front post single crochet
fptr . . . . front post treble crochet
g . . . . .gram(s)
hdc . . . . half double crochet
hdc dec . . . . .half double crochet 2 or more
stitches together, as indicated
inc . . . . increase/increases/increasing
lp(s) . . . . .loop(s)
MC . . . . .main color
mm . . . . millimeter(s)
oz . . . . .ounce(s)
pc . . . . popcorn(s)
rem . . . . .remain/remains/remaining
rep(s) . . . . .repeat(s)
rnd(s) . . . . .round(s)
RS . . . . right side
sc . . . . single crochet (singular/plural)
sc dec . . . . .single crochet 2 or more
stitches together, as indicated
sk . . . . .skip/skipped/skipping
sl st(s) . . . . slip stitch(es)
sp(s) . . . . space(s)/spaced
st(s) . . . . stitch(es)
tog . . . . .together
tr . . . . treble crochet
trtr . . . . .triple treble
WS . . . . wrong side
yd(s) . . . . .yard(s)
yo . . . . yarn over

YARN CONVERSION

OUNCES TO GRAMS		GRAMS TO OUNCES	
1	28.4	25	⅞
2	56.7	40	1⅔
3	85.0	50	1¾
4	113.4	100	3½

UNITED STATES		UNITED KINGDOM
sl st (slip stitch)	=	sc (single crochet)
sc (single crochet)	=	dc (double crochet)
hdc (half double crochet)	=	htr (half treble crochet)
dc (double crochet)	=	tr (treble crochet)
tr (treble crochet)	=	dtr (double treble crochet)
dtr (double treble crochet)	=	ttr (triple treble crochet)
skip	=	miss

Reverse single crochet (reverse sc): Ch 1, sk first st, working from left to right, insert hook in next st from front to back, draw up lp on hook, yo and draw through both lps on hook.

Chain (ch): Yo, pull through lp on hook.

Single crochet (sc): Insert hook in st; yo, pull through st, yo, pull through both lps on hook.

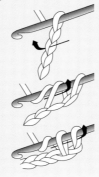

Double crochet (dc): Yo, insert hook in st, yo, pull through st, [yo, pull through 2 lps] twice.

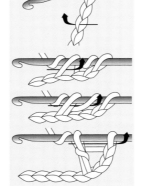

Front loop (front lp) Back loop (back lp)

Front Loop   Back Loop

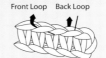

Front post stitch (fp): Back post stitch (bp): When working post st, insert hook from right to left around post of st on previous row.

Back   Front

←Post of Stitch

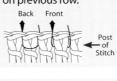

Half double crochet (hdc): Yo, insert hook in st, yo, pull through st, yo, pull through all 3 lps on hook.

Double treble crochet (dtr): Yo 3 times, insert hook in st, yo, pull through st, [yo, pull through 2 lps] 4 times.

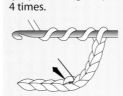

Slip stitch (sl st): Insert hook in st, pull through both lps on hook.

Chain color change (ch color change) Yo with new color, draw through last lp on hook.

Double crochet color change (dc color change) Drop first color, yo with new color, draw through last 2 lps of st.

Treble crochet (tr): Yo twice, insert hook in st, yo, pull through st, [yo, pull through 2 lps] 3 times.

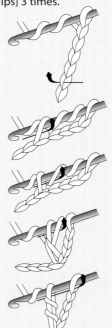

Single crochet decrease (sc dec): (Insert hook, yo, draw lp through) in each of the sts indicated, yo, draw through all lps on hook.

Example of 2-sc dec

Half double crochet decrease (hdc dec): (Yo, insert hook, yo, draw lp through) in each of the sts indicated, yo, draw through all lps on hook.

Example of 2-hdc dec

Double crochet decrease (dc dec): (Yo, insert hook, yo, draw lp through, yo, draw through 2 lps on hook) in each of the sts indicated, yo, draw through all lps on hook.

Example of 2-dc dec

Treble crochet decrease (tr dec): Holding back last lp of each st, tr in each of the sts indicated, yo, pull through all lps on hook.

Example of 2-tr dec

Metric
Conversion
Charts

METRIC CONVERSIONS

yards	x	.9144	=	metres (m)
yards	x	91.44	=	centimetres (cm)
inches	x	2.54	=	centimetres (cm)
inches	x	25.40	=	millimetres (mm)
inches	x	.0254	=	metres (m)

centimetres	x	.3937	=	inches
metres	x	1.0936	=	yards

INCHES INTO MILLIMETRES & CENTIMETRES (Rounded off slightly)

inches	mm	cm	inches	cm	inches	cm	inches	cm
1/8	3	0.3	5	12.5	21	53.5	38	96.5
1/4	6	0.6	5 1/2	14	22	56	39	99
3/8	10	1	6	15	23	58.5	40	101.5
1/2	13	1.3	7	18	24	61	41	104
5/8	15	1.5	8	20.5	25	63.5	42	106.5
3/4	20	2	9	23	26	66	43	109
7/8	22	2.2	10	25.5	27	68.5	44	112
1	25	2.5	11	28	28	71	45	114.5
1 1/4	32	3.2	12	30.5	29	73.5	46	117
1 1/2	38	3.8	13	33	30	76	47	119.5
1 3/4	45	4.5	14	35.5	31	79	48	122
2	50	5	15	38	32	81.5	49	124.5
2 1/2	65	6.5	16	40.5	33	84	50	127
3	75	7.5	17	43	34	86.5		
3 1/2	90	9	18	46	35	89		
4	100	10	19	48.5	36	91.5		
4 1/2	115	11.5	20	51	37	94		

KNITTING NEEDLES CONVERSION CHART

Canada/U.S.	0	1	2	3	4	5	6	7	8	9	10	10½	11	13	15
Metric (mm)	2	2¼	2¾	3¼	3½	3¾	4	4½	5	5½	6	6½	8	9	10

CROCHET HOOKS CONVERSION CHART

Canada/U.S.	1/B	2/C	3/D	4/E	5/F	6/G	8/H	9/I	10/J	10½/K	N
Metric (mm)	2.25	2.75	3.25	3.5	3.75	4.25	5	5.5	6	6.5	9.0

Annie's®

Lots to Love Cute As Pie 5" Doll Clothes is published by Annie's, 306 East Parr Road, Berne, IN 46711. Printed in USA. Copyright © 2013 Annie's. All rights reserved. This publication may not be reproduced in part or in whole without written permission from the publisher.

RETAIL STORES: If you would like to carry this pattern book or any other Annie's publication, visit AnniesWSL.com

Every effort has been made to ensure that the instructions in this pattern book are complete and accurate. We cannot, however, take responsibility for human error, typographical mistakes or variations in individual work. Please visit AnniesCustomerCare.com to check for pattern updates.

ISBN: 978-1-59635-846-1

1 2 3 4 5 6 7 8 9